MW01610677

101
KIWIFRUIT IDEAS

R&R PUBLISHING

R&R Publishing
First published in 1993 by
R&R Publishing
12 Treeview Place, Epping, NSW 2121
Telephone (02) 876 5958 Facsimile (02) 876 3782

Publisher: Richard Carroll
Recipe Research: Terry Morrison
Jan Bilton
Data Entry: Sean McNamara
Cover Design: Jon Terpstra
Photography: New Zealand Kiwifruit Marketing Board
Proof Reading: Jackie Dettmann

The National Library of Australia
Cataloguing-in-Publication Data

Includes index.
ISBN: 1 875655 15 8

1. Cookery (Kiwifruit). 1. Title: One hundred and one kiwifruit ideas.
641.644

Printed November 1993

Computer Typeset in Times Roman by
R&R Publishing
Printed by: Pirie Printing, Canberra ACT, Australia

TABLE OF CONTENTS

INTRODUCTION

Welcome to New Zealand kiwifruit, "The world's finest".

New Zealand is acknowledged as the world leader in kiwifruit, setting the standards in research, production, post harvest operations, packaging, distribution, marketing and quality of customer service.

New Zealand pioneered today's international kiwifruit industry, building on that heritage to retain its position as world leader against competitors.

We are practical, down to earth people, who tend out beautiful, green, pollution-free land to grow superb quality kiwifruit. We are also innovators who continually work to improve the way we do things to meet the needs of customers all over the world.

Our growers, post-harvest operators and the New Zealand kiwifruit Marketing Board are committed to delivering not only the world's finest kiwifruit to customers but also the world's finest service.

The recipes in this book are an introduction to the exciting taste sensations of "The world's finest" kiwifruit. We hope you enjoy them.

Where do they come from?

The perfect environment for "The world's finest" kiwifruit.

Uncrowded and green, New Zealand has one of the cleanest, most pollution-free environments in the world.

The land is young, the soils have only recently been turned, and they are fertile and free draining. Bright sunshine, abundant, fresh rainfall and moderate temperatures provide the ideal conditions for growing "The world's finest" kiwifruit.

However, it is not simply the New Zealand soil and climate which are important. The people in the New Zealand kiwifruit industry bring more than 40 years' experience of crop development, research and innovation to the task of producing the perfect product.

An Italian industry representative, Mario Scianella, from the Istituto Nazionale per il Commercio Estero, said of his visit to New Zealand: "My stay was something between a dream and a reality: 10 days of adventure in a fantastic landscape, where nature has not been touched at all, fabulous beaches, a panorama variegated and always full of colours, a population of civil and well educated people, a very clean environment, not contaminated, and last but not least, wherever you look a lot of Kiwi(fruit). A country that gives you a lot of reasons to be proud."

New Zealanders invented the kiwifruit industry. They took an unculti-vated Chinese fruit and turned it into an international marketing success. New Zealand selected the commercial variety – the Hayward – and developed the skills and practices which are, today, the benchmark of the industry worldwide. In the 1950s when the first fruit was exported to England and the USA, New Zealanders chose for it a new name, kiwifruit, to identify with their country.

Roly Earp, one of the first growers to export kiwifruit, remains amazed at how immediately popular the fruit was. "We'd go overseas and look around, and suddenly kiwifruit were everywhere, even in China."

He says the initial impetus came from the growers and exporters who joined together to promote the fruit and voluntarily establish the standards of the industry. That early drive remains, Roly Earp believes, and is a characteristic of New Zealand growers. "We've always done the pioneering," he says. "The grower has an insatiable thirst for improvement."

Equally, he says, Government scientists and researchers generated a huge amount of new knowledge in the 1970s which continues even more strongly in the 1990s to give New Zealand a competitive edge. "The New Zealand industry faces major challenges as competitors seek to develop initiatives of their own. We must look to established sources of strength: the experience of people who have been in the business for 20 years or longer, and the single-seller structure of the New Zealand kiwifruit Marketing Board which sets and maintains standards and markets the products."

History of Kiwifruit in New Zealand

c1905	Chinese Gooseberry seeds are raised for the first time in New Zealand by Alexander Allison, a Wanganui nurseryman.
c1924	Hayward Wright develops the outstanding Hayward variety – now grown worldwide. Bruno Just raises his own variety "Bruno" which is today the most commonly used rootstock on to which Hayward is grafted.
1950	Widespread planting of vines in the Bay of Plenty region.
1952	First exports made.
1959	The name "Kiwifruit" first used to identify the source.
1970	NZ Kiwifruit Export Promotion Committee established.
1978	Kiwifruit Marketing Licensing Authority established to set export standards, license exporters and promote Kiwifruit internationally.
1980	The New Zealand Kiwifruit Authority replaces the KMLA.
1980s	Kiwifruit production expands significantly in Chile, Italy and France. New Zealand exports rose from 5,877 tonnes in 1977 to 185,000 tonnes in 1988.
1988	The New Zealand Kiwifruit Marketing Board is established by Government statute at the request of growers to coordinate the industry, set standards, oversee research and create a clear marketing strategy.
1991	The New Zealand brand is relaunched worldwide as "New Zealand Kiwifruit – The world's finest."

How Many Kiwifruit are Produced?

Every year more than two billion individual kiwifruit are harvested, packed, stored and shipped to more than 50 world markets. Prior to the creation of the New Zealand kiwifruit Marketing Board, the New Zealand industry was fragmented, distributing and marketing its product via several channels. Now there is coordination from the grower through to the consumer, with everyone sharing the same understanding of exactly what the customer wants and making sure it is provided to agreed quality standards. The Board provides a system of packing and handling fruit which gives the customer confidence.

It has supported the development of strong, quality relationships, based on trust and understanding. Everyone in the industry is involved, from growers and operators of packhouses and coolstores, to transport operators, shipping companies and our distributors in the markets.

Along with building strong relationships and a strong team, there's another force motivating the industry: a desire to produce a top quality product. To meet consistent quality standards and customer expectations, the Board and the industry have developed sophisticated management systems to ensure these standards are met. Every tray sold worldwide can be traced back to the original grower via the inventory system through distribution, freight, the coolstore and the packhouse.

The Board has responded to strong consumer demand for environmentally friendly packaging. New Zealand has taken the initiative in developing recyclable and reusable packs which also meet the needs of shippers, distributors and retailers. The requirement for returnable plastic containers is also being closely evaluated. The goal is to provide cost-effective packaging which minimises waste disposal in our markets and at the same time eliminates fruit handling and transit damage.

New Zealand Kiwifruit, Historical Global Exports*					
Year	Trays	Year	Trays	Year	Trays
1963	12,150	1973	367,002	1983	10,531,100
1964	21,870	1974	738,060	1984	13,736,200
1965	22,680	1975	735,399	1985	23,342,700
1966	37,800	1976	1,386,828	1986	28,901,500
1967	51,300	1977	1,675,019	1987	45,800,700
1968	73,710	1978	2,157,934	1988	49,660,900
1969	99,360	1979	4,028,242	1989	44,114,200
1970	181,800	1980	4,143,306	1990	62,788,507
1971	206,454	1981	6,213,901	1991	54,717,850
1972	264,070	1982	4,668,300	1992	52,000,000
*Includes Class I Kiwifruit only. Small quantities of New Zealand Kiwifruit have been exported since 1952					

Quality

The competition in international markets from other fresh fruit presents our industry with a challenge. However, the Board and the New Zealand kiwifruit industry are committed to maintaining the position of market leader, satisfying even the most demanding customers and their changing needs.

When it comes to special products only one country can enjoy the reputation as leader. Among wine producing nations that country is France and among cheese producers the Swiss have achieved that distinction. New Zealand has earned that reputation with kiwifruit.

International market research confirms that only New Zealand consistently produces "The world's finest" kiwifruit, quality fruit for which the consumer is prepared to pay. Market research also supports how closely all kiwifruit is associated with New Zealand kiwifruit and hence our confidence in the brand "New Zealand".

The Board's aim is to protect this brand of quality and its world leader position, and improve on it, especially in the service provided to customers. The marketing of New Zealand kiwifruit involves much more than the promotion of the name – it relies on unvarying quality of product and service to customers.

The Board has already developed a formidable reputation for distribution and service to international distributors. It ensures prompt delivery of well presented, fresh, premium grade product and has a flexible business approach driven by the ability to respond to customer requirements. Since brand-building is a long term exercise, the industry's success is based on its commitment to investment, planning and creativity at each stage from the orchard to the market.

Brand-building demands quality relationships between every person in the business. The Board is continuing to strengthen these relationships by finding out exactly what customers want and then meeting and exceeding their expectations.

New Zealand Kiwifruit	
Attributes	Produced in a pollution-free environment; moist and juicy, refreshing, sweet yet tangy.
Benefits	Easy to digest, doesn't spoil appetite, keeps you active, keeps you healthy.
Values	Makes me feel good, puts me at my best, makes me feel refreshed, makes me feel I'm taking care of myself, makes me feel I'm buying a quality product, fits my active lifestyle.
Personality	Special, fit, fresh.

Source: Brand Essence Research, February 1992.

The New Zealand Kiwifruit Marketing Board is continuously seeking to enhance the attributes of the product and the industry's competitive advantage, undertaking extensive international market research to identify new opportunities to meet customer expectations.

New Zealand invests more in research and development than any other kiwifruit producing country, and is home to many of the world's leading kiwifruit scientists. The Board directly funds more than a quarter of the $14 million spent each year on kiwifruit research to support the industry's thrust for constant improvement in every part of the business.

Areas of focus include:

• Improving the Hayward variety in terms of quality, appearance, taste and flavour, as well as developing new varieties of kiwifruit.

• Extending New Zealand's edge in producing fresh, "clean" fruit, using natural means to control orchard pests.

• Improving orchard management and post harvest techniques to achieve optimum efficiencies and maintain fruit quality.

Nutrition

Not only is kiwifruit good to eat but it's good for you.
The greatest trend in grocery shopping in the 1990s has been a swing towards fresh, unprocessed, wholesome food. Fruit and vegetables are the original convenience foods, ideal for a healthier lifestyle.

kiwifruit meets consumers' needs for health-giving food in many ways. It offers more Vitamin C than oranges or lemons; a high content of Vitamin E; a potassium content second only to bananas but with less than 40 per cent of the calories; and the fruit is one of the best sources of dietary fibre, containing fibre equivalent to four sticks of celery.

kiwifruit's outstanding nutritional quality is its very high Vitamin C content. Worldwide scientific evidence has shown that Vitamin C can actively assist in the prevention of illnesses such as cancer and heart disease. It is valuable in preventing colds and flu and healing wounds. Vitamin C and Vitamin E act as anti-oxidants, which, as well as carrying out their normal role of promoting healthy growth and healing, help fight off the destructive "free radicals" which play a major part in many diseases. Vitamin E is rarely found in other fruit, but is found in abundance in kiwifruit. It plays a vital role in the maintenance of healthy body cells, slowing the ageing process, aiding fertility and reducing the risk of heart disease.

Most Western diets are low in fibre. kiwifruit is full of fibre and this can help lower cholesterol levels, keep bodily functions regular and reduce the risk of bowel cancer. This health capsule is also a good source of minerals such as potassium, magnesium, calcium and phosphorous. Additional health benefits of kiwifruit are that it is low in fat, cholesterol, calories, starch and sodium.

kiwifruit can be a significant, healthy part of the daily diet. It is no surprise we are making sure New Zealand kiwifruit offers the finest guarantee of freshness, nutrition and vitality!

Vitamin C Content of Popular Fruits*

Kiwifruit	85
Strawberry	60
Orange	50
Tomato	25
Banana	12.5
Apple	6
Grape	6
Peach	5
Pear	4

*mg/100g of fresh weight edible portion.

Calorie Count of Selected Fruits*

Avocado	161
Banana	92
Grape	63
Kiwifruit	61

*Calories per 100g fresh weight edible portion.

AVOCADO WITH KIWI

INGREDIENTS

2 avocados
2 New Zealand Kiwifruit
1 tablespoon finely diced
    red pepper (capsicum)
½ cup bean sprouts

grated rind of ½ lemon
½ teaspoon grated root ginger
freshly ground black pepper
3 teaspoons lemon juice

METHOD

Halve the avocados and remove the stones. Peel and dice Kiwifruit and combine carefully with remaining ingredients. Spoon into centre of avocados and serve.

SERVES 4

EGGPLANT KIWI AND PESTO SANDWICH

INGREDIENTS

2 medium eggplants (aubergine)
salt
oil for frying
3 New Zealand Kiwifruit
6 slices goat's milk Camembert
    or fresh Mozzarella

8 tablespoons pesto
fresh herbs e.g. basil, rocket or mint
6 slices red pepper (capsicum)
6 tablespoons balsamic vinegar

METHOD

Cut the eggplant into thick slices and sprinkle with salt. Stand for 2 hours. Pat dry with paper towels. Pan-fry the eggplant slices in shallow oil until golden brown on both sides. Drain and pat dry on paper towels.

Meanwhile, peel and slice the Kiwifruit.

To serve, place a slice of eggplant on each plate and top with a slice of cheese. Cover the cheese with Kiwifruit and 1 tablespoon of pesto. Sprinkle with a few coarsely chopped herbs and add a teaspoon of vinegar. Cover with another slice of eggplant and finish with a little pesto and a few herbs on top. Serve at once.

SERVES 6

GIANT FRUIT WONTONS WITH MIXED FRUIT PURÉE

INGREDIENTS

6 spring roll wrappers
1 large banana
1 tablespoon lemon juice
4 New Zealand Kiwifruit

½ cup raspberries or similar
oil for frying
caster (superfine) sugar

METHOD

Peel and cut the banana in 2cm (¾") cubes. Take two Kiwifruit and cut in similar size pieces. Combine with lemon juice and banana.

Place a little of the fruit filling on one side of the wrapper leaving 2cm free either side of the filling. Roll up leaving a little of the wrapper unrolled at the end. Pull ends around until they slightly overlap the tube. Pinch together. Repeat with remaining wrappers.

Purée remaining Kiwifruit and raspberries separately.

Just before serving heat oil until a faint haze rises. Deep fry wontons quickly one or two at a time until golden. Drain on paper towels. Spoon a little of the two purées onto six serving plates and add wontons. Dust with sugar before serving.

SERVES 6

KIWI BRUSCHETTA

INGREDIENTS

1 baguette loaf
2-3 tablespoons olive oil
3 New Zealand Kiwifruit

2 medium tomatoes
250g mozzarella cheese
fresh basil leaves (15-20)

METHOD

Cut baguette into 1cm (½ inch) slices. Brush slices on both sides with olive oil and place on cookie sheet. Toast at 200°C, until golden, about 10 minutes (toast rounds may be made in advance and stored in airtight container). Wash and trim ends from Kiwifruit. Cut into thin slices. Thinly slice tomatoes; cut each slice in half. Using a cheese slicer or shaver, thinly slice mozzarella. To assemble, arrange mozzarella, basil leaf, tomato and Kiwifruit on top of each baguette slice. Makes 25 to 30 bruschetta.

SERVES 8-10

KIWI SHRIMP COCKTAIL

INGREDIENTS

1 tablespoon crème fraîche (30% fat)
lemon juice
pepper from the mill
dill

75g shrimps
mesclun (mixed salad)
1 New Zealand Kiwifruit (75g)
1 slice wholemeal bread (40g)

METHOD

Mix the crème fraîche with some lemon juice. Season with pepper and finely cut dill. Mix in the shrimps. Spread a cocktail bowl with mesclun leaves. Fill in the shrimp salad and put it in the refrigerator. Meanwhile, peel the New Zealand Kiwifruit, cut it into thin slices and cut these into halves. Before serving, mix them under the shrimp cocktail. Eat with wholemeal bread (toasted in a toaster or a coated pan).

SERVES 1

KIWICADO STARTER

INGREDIENTS

2 avocados

3 New Zealand Kiwifruit

2 tablespoons each chopped mint, basil, lemon grass, coriander

salt and pepper

1 teaspoon each diced chilli, garlic, root ginger

1 tablespoon each thick soy sauce, lemon juice

METHOD

Halve the avocados and remove stones. Carefully scoop out flesh then cut in 2cm cubes. Peel and cut Kiwifruit in a similar size. Combine the avocado and Kiwifruit with all herbs, salt and pepper. Carefully spoon back into the shells.

Combine all other ingredients and serve on or with the starter.

A popular Indonesian recipe.

SERVES 4

KIWI SUMMER SOUP

INGREDIENTS

2 cups pineapple juice
½ cup sugar
juice and finely grated rind
   1 lemon
4 New Zealand Kiwifruit

pulp 2 passionfruit
1 cup raspberries or small
   strawberries
1 cup blackberries or blueberries
2 New Zealand Kiwifruit, extra

METHOD

Combine pineapple juice, sugar, lemon juice and rind in a saucepan and bring to the boil. Stir well. Cool.

Peel and chop Kiwifruit. Purée until just smooth, sieve to remove seeds. Stir into pineapple mixture. Add passionfruit pulp. Chill.

Before serving add berries and Kiwifruit cut into balls with a melon baller.

SERVES 6

KIWI TACO

INGREDIENTS
5 taco shells
1 onion, sliced
3 New Zealand Kiwifruit,
   peeled and sliced
1 large avocado, stoned and sliced

1 large tomato
1 small chilli, diced
1 teaspoon oil
salt and pepper
4 tablespoons sour cream

METHOD
Crisp taco shells in oven if necessary. Fill with onion, Kiwifruit and avocado. Combine tomato, chilli, oil and seasonings. Spoon on top of tacos with sour cream.

MAKES 5

MARINATED MOZZARELLA OLIVES & KIWIFRUIT

INGREDIENTS

250g Mozzarella cheese
4 New Zealand Kiwifruit,
    peeled and sliced
2 tablespoons mixed fresh herbs
3 tablespoons olive oil

2 tablespoons salad oil
1 clove garlic, crushed
salt and pepper
black olives

METHOD

Thinly slice mozzarella and layer with Kiwifruit on a serving plate. Whisk herbs, oils, garlic, salt and pepper and sprinkle over the cheese and Kiwifruit. Marinate 30 minutes. Top with olives and serve with crusty bread. Makes a great starter or light meal.

SERVES 4

NEW ZEALAND KIWIFRUIT WITH HAM MAYONNAISE

INGREDIENTS

4 small New Zealand Kiwifruit
lemon juice
black pepper
4 slices honey roast ham, halved

4 tablespoons mayonnaise
chopped parsley
bread sticks

METHOD

Peel and thinly slice the Kiwifruit. Squeeze lemon juice over and add a turn or two of fresh ground pepper. Roll up 4 halves of ham and cut into twelve 2.5cm (1 inch) rolls. Arrange the remaining ham and Kiwifruit on 4 plates. Garnish with ham rolls, mayonnaise and chopped parsley. Serve accompanied with bread sticks.

Note: This beautifully simple food makes a good lunch dish. Ring the changes with a curried mayonnaise.

SERVES 4

SALMON TOAST WITH
NEW ZEALAND KIWIFRUIT

INGREDIENTS

2 New Zealand Kiwifruit
40g softened butter
1 teaspoon horseradish sauce

4 slices of rye toast
4 slices of salmon (approx. 30g)
lemon balm of dill for decoration

METHOD

Peel the Kiwifruit and stew one half of it. Mix it with the butter and the horseradish. Roast the toast and spread it with the kiwi-horseradish-butter. Put the salmon slices on top. Cut the remaining Kiwifruit into slices, divide these into four parts and put them onto the salmon. Decorate with lemon balm of dill.

SERVES 4

SPICY KIWI PIZZA

INGREDIENTS

1 pita bread
2 tablespoons chilli tomato sauce
1 teaspoon chopped fresh oregano
50g sliced pepperoni sausage,
    finely shredded
¼ red pepper (capsicum), finely
    sliced

1 New Zealand Kiwifruit, peeled
    and sliced
3 black olives
½ cup grated Mozzarella cheese
1 teaspoon grated Parmesan cheese

METHOD

Brush chilli sauce over the pita bread base, sprinkle with oregano and
remaining ingredients.

Cook under hot grill for 4 minutes or until cheese has melted. Sprinkle
with Parmesan cheese.

SERVES 1

SWISS STYLE MUESLI

INGREDIENTS

1 cup rolled oats
2 tablespoons lemon juice
2 tablespoons liquid honey
½ cup cold water

2 tablespoons chopped hazelnuts
2 New Zealand Kiwifruit, peeled
   and diced

METHOD

Place rolled oats in a bowl. Combine lemon juice, honey and water. Warm until honey is melted. Stir into rolled oats with hazelnuts. Leave 1 hour or overnight. Before serving add the Kiwifruit.

SERVES 2

TAPAS

INGREDIENTS

Kiwi Mussels:
4 large steamed mussels in shells
1 New Zealand Kiwifruit
1 tablespoon each balsamic
    vinegar, olive oil

Kiwi Venison:
4 thin slices rare venison
1 tablespoon each olive oil, wine
    vinegar
4 slices New Zealand Kiwifruit
4 cocktail rounds

Kiwi Lamb:
200g lean minced lamb
1 teaspoon grated root ginger
4 slices New Zealand Kiwifruit
4 slices French stick

Kiwi Salmon:
4 slices smoked salmon
lemon juice
freshly ground black pepper
4 slices New Zealand Kiwifruit,
    halved

METHOD

Kiwi Mussels: Discard one half of each shell. Remove mussels from shells, and dice. Combine with diced Kiwifruit, vinegar and oil and replace in the shell.

Kiwi Venison: Dip venison into oil and vinegar combined. Place Kiwifruit on cocktail rounds and top with venison.

Kiwi Lamb: Mix lamb with ginger and form in four small patties. Briefly grill both sides. Place on a round of Kiwifruit on a slice of French bread.

Kiwi Salmon: Sprinkle salmon with lemon juice and pepper. Skewer on four cocktail sticks with Kiwifruit.

SERVES 4

23

CHARGRILLED FISH WITH KIWIFRUIT AND DILL

INGREDIENTS

500g white fish
olive oil
1 firm tomato
1 small red onion, diced
2-3 teaspoons chopped dill

3-4 New Zealand Kiwifruit, peeled
    and sliced
3 teaspoons chopped dill, extra
black olives, optional

METHOD

Cut slits in the fish on both sides. Brush with olive oil. Grill one side for 2 minutes. Turn fish over.

Place sliced tomato in slits and sprinkle with onion, dill and a little more oil. Grill 3 minutes until cooked. Insert sliced Kiwifruit in slits and grill 1 minute.

Serve with diced Kiwifruit on the side mixed with chopped dill and black olives.

Use whole fish if desired.

SERVES 4

CHARGRILLED SALMON WITH KIWIFRUIT MINT RELISH

INGREDIENTS

4 salmon steaks, or substitute
    swordfish or grouper (hapuka)
juice and grated rind of 1 lemon
2 tablespoons oil

Kiwifruit Mint Relish:
2 tablespoons cider vinegar
1 tablespoon smooth Dijon
    mustard
1 tablespoon honey
freshly ground black pepper
4 New Zealand Kiwifruit
½ cup coarsely chopped fresh
    mint leaves

METHOD

Brush fish both sides with combined juice, rind and oil. Refrigerate while preparing the relish.

Mix vinegar, mustard, honey and black pepper together. Combine with sliced Kiwifruit and mint leaves.

Cook fish over a grill about 3 minutes each side, brushing with more lemon mixture on turning. Serve with the fresh relish.

SERVES 4

CRISPY FISH WITH KIWIFRUIT MINT SAMBAL

INGREDIENTS

¾ cup chickpea flour
2 teaspoons garam masala
½-1 teaspoon chilli powder
½ teaspoon salt
¾ cup water
1 tablespoon oil
1 egg white
500g white fish fillets, skinned

1 teaspoon salt
1 tablespoon lime or lemon juice
oil for deep frying
Sambal:
2 large New Zealand Kiwifruit
2 tablespoons chopped fresh mint
1 teaspoon grated root ginger

METHOD

Combine chickpea flour, garam masala, chilli powder, and salt then gradually beat in the water. Stand for 30 minutes. Beat in 1 tablespoon oil. Whip egg white then fold in batter.

Rub fish with salt and lime juice and leave to stand 15 minutes. Dry the fish, divide in serving size pieces then dip in batter and deep fry about 1 minute until crisp. Serve with Kiwifruit and mint sambal.

To prepare sambal, peel and cut fruit in large dice. Add mint and ginger.

SERVES 4

JADE PRAWNS

INGREDIENTS

2 tablespoons oil
500g raw prawns
2 tablespoons each chopped fresh
    coriander (cilantro), parsley,
    basil

2 cloves garlic, chopped
3 tablespoons chopped spring
    onions (scallions)
salt and pepper
2 large New Zealand Kiwifruit,
    diced

METHOD

Heat oil in a wok or large frying pan. Add the prawns and all remaining
ingredients except Kiwifruit. Stir-fry over high heat 5-7 minutes. Add
Kiwifruit, cook 1 minute then serve immediately.

SERVES 4

MARINATED FISH WITH RICE VINEGAR

INGREDIENTS

500g lean boneless fish (ling, black dory, tuna, other white fish)

½ cup rice vinegar

2 tablespoons light soy sauce

1 red onion, diced

2 tablespoons chopped coriander (cilantro)

3 New Zealand Kiwifruit, peeled and diced

METHOD

Cut fish in 2.5cm (1") cubes. Place in a glass bowl and cover with rice vinegar and soy combined. Stir to coat. Marinate in refrigerator for several hours, stirring occasionally.

Drain and mix with remaining ingredients and serve.

SERVES 4

PEPPERED PRAWNS

INGREDIENTS

18 green prawns
¼ cup lime juice
freshly ground black pepper

Sauce:
3 New Zealand Kiwifruit
1 chilli, chopped
½ teaspoon coarsely ground black
    pepper
2 tablespoons roasted peanuts,
    finely chopped

METHOD

Shell the prawns but leave the tails on. Place each prawn on long bamboo
skewers. Sprinkle with lime juice. Just before cooking sprinkle with
black pepper and grill or cook over hot coals.

Serve with the sauce. Peel and dice the Kiwifruit. Add the other ingredients and serve immediately.

SERVES 6

PRAWN CURRY

INGREDIENTS

500g prawns
1 tablespoon ghee or butter
1 onion, sliced
1 teaspoon each ground turmeric,
    sugar
½-1 teaspoon chilli powder
2 tablespoons garam masala

2 New Zealand Kiwifruit, peeled
    and chopped
¾ cup water
salt and pepper
extra Kiwifruit for garnish
boiled rice

METHOD

Peel prawns and set aside. Heat ghee and gently fry onion until soft and beginning to turn golden. Mix turmeric, sugar, chilli and garam masala to a stiff paste with a little cold water and add to onions. Fry, stirring frequently for 2-3 minutes.

Add Kiwifruit and cook until soft and pulpy. Add water and simmer uncovered for 10 minutes. Place prawns, salt and pepper into the pan and cook until prawns are hot. Peel and dice Kiwifruit and serve with the prawns and rice.

SERVES 4

SPICY RICE WITH KIWI

INGREDIENTS

150g raw prawns*
1 medium onion
2 cloves garlic
2 teaspoons each grated root
  ginger, diced chilli
½ teaspoon dried shrimp paste
  (trasi), optional

oil for frying
3 cups cold cooked rice
2 spring onions, sliced
1 tablespoon soy sauce
2 New Zealand Kiwifruit, sliced

METHOD

Shell and devein the prawns. Chop onions and place in a blender with garlic, ginger, chilli and shrimp paste. Purée.

Heat 2 tablespoons oil in a wok or frypan and cook the blended ingredients briefly. Add the prawns or meat and stir-fry until cooked. Add a little more oil, the rice and spring onions, tossing and mixing until very hot. Sprinkle with soy sauce. Serve the rice topped with Kiwifruit and strips of omelette. May be garnished with chillies.

*This recipe can also be made substituting 150g of beef steak cut into thin strips.

SERVES 4

STEAMED SHELLFISH WITH FRUIT VINEGAR

INGREDIENTS

48 clams, cockles or small
    mussels
4 shallots, diced
¼ cup raspberry vinegar or
    similar
¼ cup water

1 tablespoon olive oil
3 New Zealand Kiwifruit, peeled
    and diced
½ cup raspberries
salt and pepper

METHOD

Wash shellfish well and scrub. Remove beards if necessary.

Place in a large pan with shallots, vinegar and water. Cover and simmer until shells open about 5 minutes. Discard any that do not open.

Place shellfish in a bowl. Strain cooking liquid and add oil. Sprinkle over the mussels with Kiwifruit and raspberries.

SERVES 6

BEEF MEDALLIONS WITH
KIWI PEPPER SAUCE

INGREDIENTS

2 small potatoes (125g)
2 thin slices beef fillet (60g)
1 teaspoon butter or margarine
salt
pepper from the mill
2 tablespoons dry white wine

1 tablespoon crème fraîche
  (30% fat)
1 teaspoon pickled green
  peppercorns (5g)
1 New Zealand Kiwifruit (75g)

METHOD

Peel the potatoes and cook them in a little salted water for approx. 20 minutes. Heat the butter in a coated pan. Fry the medallions on both sides for 2 minutes each, season and wrap them in aluminium foil. Loosen the meat sauce with white wine and mix in the crème fraîche. Add the peppercorns and heat up the sauce shortly once more. Peel the New Zealand Kiwifruit, cut it into slices, quarters or eighths. Add them at last and heat them shortly. Serve the medallions with the sauce and the potatoes.

SERVES 2

MARINATED BEEF, KIWIFRUIT AND SESAME

INGREDIENTS

1kg lean rump steak

Marinade:

3 tablespoons soy sauce

2 teaspoons sesame oil

2 tablespoons each water, rice
   vinegar

1 teaspoon roasted ground
   sesame seeds

1 clove garlic, crushed

2 teaspoons sugar

Side dish:

4 New Zealand Kiwifruit, peeled
   and diced

1 teaspoon sesame oil

1 tablespoon sesame seeds

Garnish:

16 trimmed lettuce leaves

METHOD

Slice beef thinly. Combine all ingredients for marinade and marinate beef
for at least 3 hours.

Combine Kiwifruit with oil and seeds. Trim lettuce to make cups to hold
meat and Kiwifruit.

Barbecue or grill steak quickly until just cooked. To serve, place small
amounts in the lettuce then add the Kiwifruit.

SERVES 6-8

RED BEEF AND KIWI

INGREDIENTS

500g lean rump (grilling) steak
2 tablespoons cooking oil
1 teaspoon sliced root ginger
1 clove garlic, crushed
1 red pepper (capsicum), sliced

1 teaspoon hoisin sauce
2 New Zealand Kiwifruit, peeled
   and sliced
1 cup crispy noodles

METHOD

Thinly slice the meat. Heat oil in a wok or frypan and stir-fry ginger and garlic 30 seconds. Add meat in batches, stir-frying until just cooked, about 1 minute. Remove meat to one side.

Stir-fry the pepper 1 minute. Combine meat with hoisin sauce then return to the pan and quickly heat through. Add the Kiwifruit and crispy noodles and serve.

SERVES 4

SLICED BEEF WITH KIWIFRUIT

INGREDIENTS

500g lean frying steak

1 onion, chopped

4 cloves garlic

1 teaspoon coarsely ground
    pepper

3 tablespoons dark soy sauce

2 tablespoons palm or brown sugar

2 tablespoons peanut oil

2 New Zealand Kiwifruit, peeled
    and diced

METHOD

Flatten the meat so it is very thin. Place onion, garlic, pepper, soy sauce
and sugar into an electric blender and purée. Marinate the meat in this
mixture for 1 hour. Drain well.

Heat oil in a wok or frypan and stir-fry meat in batches. Add the Kiwifruit
and serve. May be topped with diced tomato and chilli.

SERVES 4

LAMB CHOPS WITH NEW ZEALAND KIWIFRUIT-PUMPKIN DRESSING

INGREDIENTS

8 double lamb chops (2cm thick)
2 tablespoons oil
2 pinches ground rosemary
1 pinch garlic powder
freshly ground pepper
2 New Zealand Kiwifruit
80g pumpkin compote (freshly
    cooked or from jar)

salt
sugar
white pepper

Decoration:
3 New Zealand Kiwifruit
4 bouquets mint

METHOD

Wash the lamb chops and dab them dry. Mix the oil with the rosemary, the garlic and the pepper. Marinate the lamb cutlets for ½ hour. Meanwhile, peel the Kiwifruit, cut them and mash them with a fork. Add 2 tablespoons of pumpkin compote juice. Cut the pumpkin pieces and put them in the dressing and season it. Fry the lamb chops (3 minutes each side). Peel the remaining Kiwifruit and cut them in half and whole slices. Arrange the meat on the Kiwifruit sauce and decorate with Kiwifruit slices.

SERVES 4

LAMB IN PITA POCKETS WITH CITRON SALSA

INGREDIENTS

500g lean lamb
1 clove garlic, crushed
¼ cup each oil, lemon juice
4 small pita (Lebanese) breads
1 red pepper (capsicum),
    thinly sliced
salad leaves

Citron salsa:
finely grated rind 2 lemons
3 New Zealand Kiwifruit
1 small tomato, diced
1 tablespoon chopped fresh
    coriander (cilantro) or mint

METHOD

Marinate lamb in the piece in combined garlic, oil and lemon juice for at least 3 hours.

Drain well then roast or grill for about 20 minutes per 500g at 190°C.

Meanwhile warm the pocket bread. The bread may be filled or topped with salad leaves then with pepper and lamb. Combine the rind with the peeled and finely diced Kiwifruit, tomato and coriander. Serve as a topping for the lamb.

SERVES 4

MARINATED LAMB, LEMON AND KIWI

INGREDIENTS

500g boneless lamb
¼ cup lemon juice
1 tablespoon chopped rosemary
2 tablespoons olive oil

1 lemon, thinly sliced
4 prunes
3 New Zealand Kiwifruit, peeled
  and sliced

METHOD

Slice meat if thick. Place in a dish. Whisk juice, oil and rosemary and pour over meat. Add lemon slices, prunes and Kiwifruit. Cover, refrigerate and marinate for 30 minutes.

Remove meat from marinade. Cook under a preheated grill 3-4 minutes each side, depending on thickness, until just cooked inside. Slice onto a serving platter. Heat marinade ingredients briefly then serve as a sauce with the lamb.

SERVES 4

PINE NUT LAMB AND KIWIFRUIT MEZZEH

INGREDIENTS

1 onion, diced
1 tablespoon oil
500g lean minced lamb
1 egg
2 tablespoons pine nuts (pine
    kernels), chopped
salt and pepper
¼ teaspoon ground cumin

Kiwifruit Pickle:
3 New Zealand Kiwifruit
6 tablespoons finely chopped
    walnuts
½ teaspoon salt
1 teaspoon ground paprika
zest and juice 1 lemon
2-3 teaspoons olive oil

Yoghurt and Kiwi Salad:
1 cup plain yoghurt
¼ teaspoon salt
1 clove garlic, crushed
2 New Zealand Kiwifruit, peeled
    and diced
2 tablespoons fresh mint
honey to taste
diced red pepper (capsicum) for
    garnish

METHOD

Sauté the onion in the oil until soft then add to all other ingredients. Shape mixture into 2cm balls. Either poach in broth for about 20 minutes or pan fry in a little oil (or grill) for 10 minutes turning often. Serve with the following New Zealand Kiwifruit accompaniments.

Kiwifruit Pickle: Peel and cut Kiwifruit into 1cm cubes. Add the walnuts, salt, paprika, lemon. Mix with olive oil and serve.

Yoghurt and Kiwi Salad: Place the yoghurt in a bowl with salt, garlic, Kiwifruit and mint. Serve garnished with red pepper.

SERVES 4

YOGHURT MARINATED LAMB

INGREDIENTS

500g lean lamb steak
1 New Zealand Kiwifruit, mashed
½ cup plain yoghurt
2 teaspoons ground cumin
1 teaspoon mustard seeds
1 teaspoon ground black pepper

¼ teaspoon ground cardamom
Sauce:
3 New Zealand Kiwifruit, puréed
1 teaspoon mustard seeds
½ teaspoon ground cumin

METHOD

Trim lamb and "fork" the meat to help the tenderising effect of the Kiwifruit. Spoon a little pulp on a plate, top with meat and cover with remaining pulp. Stand for 30 minutes.

Remove meat and pat dry. Cut in cubes and thread on skewers.

Combine yoghurt, cumin, mustard seeds, pepper and cardamom and brush over meat. Stand for 30 minutes if required.

Place under a hot grill for 4-5 minutes each side.

Meanwhile, combine Kiwifruit purée, mustard seeds and cumin for sauce. Serve with the cooked skewers of meat.

SERVES 4

LAMB CUTLETS WITH GINGER AND KIWIFRUIT SAUCE

INGREDIENTS

1-2 large lamb racks, chined
oil
salt and pepper

Sauce:
1 cup beef consomme or good
    beef stock
2 tablespoons sugar
1½ tablespoons finely shredded
    root ginger
3 large New Zealand Kiwifruit
1 tablespoon green peppercorns
    in brine

METHOD

Place racks in a roasting pan and brush with oil. Sprinkle with salt and pepper. Roast at 200°C for about 10-15 minutes per 500g. The meat should still be a little pink inside.

Meanwhile prepare the sauce. Boil stock, sugar and vinegar until stock is reduced by about one third. Peel Kiwifruit. Pulp one Kiwifruit and sieve. Add to the sauce.

Slice remaining fruit. Just before serving, add sliced fruit and heat through about 1 minute. The fruit should still be green. Add rinsed and drained peppercorns. Spoon sauce over the meat to serve.

Allow about 2-3 cutlets per person depending on size

APPLE KIWI LIVER WITH MARJORAM

INGREDIENTS

1 small apple (100g)	salt
1 New Zealand Kiwifruit (75g)	pepper
125g veal liver	marjoram
2 teaspoons butter or margarine	dry white wine

METHOD

Remove the kernels from the apple with an apple corer and cut the apple into thin rings. Peel the New Zealand Kiwifruit and cut it into slices. Remove the tendons from the veal liver. Rinse it shortly in cold water and dab it dry with kitchen crèpe. Heat 1 teaspoon butter or margarine in a coated pan. Fry the liver at low temperature on both sides for 2 minutes each. Salt, pepper and keep warm. Add the remaining butter to the frying fat and melt it. Add the apple rings and fry them for 2-3 minutes, keep stirring. Add the New Zealand Kiwifruit and some wine. Heat shortly. Add the liver, season with finely cut marjoram. Serve hot.

SERVES 2

BROCHETTE OF PORK AND
NEW ZEALAND KIWIFRUIT

INGREDIENTS

550g boneless pork
4 New Zealand Kiwifruit
45ml corn oil
15ml lemon juice
45ml Worcestershire sauce

5ml whole grain mustard
5ml ground cumin
salt and pepper
1 red pepper

METHOD

Cut the pork into neat pieces about 2cm (1 inch) cubes. Peel and mash two
Kiwifruit. Put purée into a bowl with the corn oil, lemon juice, Worcestershire sauce, mustard and cumin. Mix well and season. Pour over the
pork and leave to marinate for ½ hour only. Arrange the pork on oiled
skewers (ideally bamboo sticks), alternating with squares of blanched red
pepper. Grill for 10 minutes. Turn halfway through cooking and brush
with remaining marinade. To serve, finish each skewer with wedges of
the reserved peeled Kiwifruit.

Note: This dish does not take long to prepare but looks fantastic and tastes
superb. Choose Kiwifruit which are on the firm side; it is important to
leave the pork in the marinade for half an hour only before cooking.

SERVES 4

KIWI TURKEY CURRY WITH RICE

INGREDIENTS

2 tablespoons rice (25g)
1 small turkey fillet (125g)
salt
pepper
curry

1 teaspoon butter or margarine
2 tablespoons dry white wine
1 tablespoon crème fraîche
  (30% fat)
1 New Zealand Kiwifruit (75g)

METHOD

Cook the rice according to instructions. Rub the turkey fillet on all sides with a little salt, pepper and curry and cut it into fine strips. Heat the butter in a coated pan. Put in the turkey fillet and fry it for 3-4 minutes, keep stirring. Add the wine and loosen the meat sauce. Mix in the crème fraîche and season with curry. Peel the New Zealand Kiwifruit and cut it into slices, halves or quarters. Add it at last and heat it up shortly. Serve with rice.

SERVES 2

NEW ZEALAND KIWIFRUIT AND TURKEY PIE

INGREDIENTS

3 slices deep-frozen puff pastry
    (180g)
500g turkey fillet
1 onion
200g fresh mushrooms
2 New Zealand Kiwifruit
    (approx. 100g each)

50g butter or margarine
salt
pepper
3 tablespoons white wine
2 tablespoons crème fraîche
1 egg yolk

METHOD

Defrost the puff pastry according to instructions. Cut the turkey fillet into very thin pieces. Peel the onion and cut it into small cubes. Clean, wash and cut the mushrooms. Peel the Kiwifruit, cut them into quarters or pieces. Heat the oven at 210-220°C. Heat some of the butter in a large pan, put in the turkey, fry and keep turning it at high temperature for 2-3 minutes. Add the onion and stew it shortly. Season with salt, herb pepper and soy sauce and complete with wine and crème fraîche. Take the pan from the stove. Heat the remaining butter in a pot and stew the mushrooms in it, then add them to the meat. If necessary, add more seasoning. Finally, mix in the prepared Kiwifruit. Pour the mixture into pie-mould (approx. diameter 27cm). Put the defrosted puff pastry slices on top of each other and roll them out, a little bigger than the pie mould. Cover the mould with the pastry and tighten it thoroughly at the inner frame. Stir the yolk, spread it on the pastry cover and pierce it several times with a fork. Bake the turkey pie in the preheated oven for approx. 20-25 minutes until it turns golden brown.

SERVES 4

PHEASANT ORANGE AND KIWIFRUIT

INGREDIENTS

1.5kg pheasant
1 tablespoon cooking oil
2 tablespoons orange juice
salt and pepper
3-4 New Zealand Kiwifruit

Orange Sauce:
1 orange
1 tablespoon cornflour
2 tablespoons sugar
1 cup fresh orange juice
2 tablespoons cider vinegar

METHOD

Prepare and truss pheasant for cooking. Brush with oil and orange juice and sprinkle with salt and pepper. Place on a rack in a roasting pan, cover loosely with foil and roast at 160˚C for 20 minutes per 500g. Remove foil during last 20 minutes of cooking.

Peel Kiwifruit and using a melon baller make balls of Kiwifruit.

To make sauce, cut orange peel in thin julienne strips. Combine cornflour and sugar with the peel then stir in orange juice and vinegar. Stir over low heat until thick. Add Kiwifruit to sauce just before serving.

SERVES 6

VENISON WITH KIWIFRUIT AND CHERRY SAUCE

INGREDIENTS

750g boneless venison grilling
  steak
1 tablespoon each smooth
  mustard, honey, chopped
  rosemary, parsley

Kiwifruit and Cherry Sauce:
1 cup red wine
¼ cup lemon juice
1 tablespoon each sugar, cornflour
  (cornstarch)
¼ cup water
finely grated rind 1 lemon
salt and pepper
3 New Zealand Kiwifruit, peeled
  and sliced
1 cup cherries, fresh or frozen

METHOD

Brush venison with mustard and honey combined. Grill about 5-8
minutes each side depending on thickness. Baste during cooking and
sprinkle with herbs at the end.

To make sauce, combine wine, lemon juice, sugar and cornflour mixed
with water. Cook over low heat stirring until thickened. Season with
lemon, salt and pepper. Add Kiwifruit and cherries just before serving.
Serve with thinly sliced venison.

SERVES 8

CHICKEN WITH CURRY DRESSING AND KIWIFRUIT

INGREDIENTS

1kg cooked chicken
1 tablespoon oil
1 medium onion, chopped
1 tablespoon curry powder

4 New Zealand Kiwifruit
¼ cup mayonnaise
¼ cup yoghurt
25g toasted almonds in skin

METHOD

Remove bones and skin from chicken. Slice meat thinly.

Heat oil in a small frypan, add onion and cook until clear. Add curry powder and cook another 3 minutes. Cool.

Peel and slice 3 Kiwifruit. Combine with onions, mayonnaise, yoghurt and chicken. Serve garnished with slices of Kiwifruit and almonds.

SERVES 4

GLAZED CHICKEN, KUMQUATS AND KIWI

INGREDIENTS

1kg chicken portions
salt
½ cup orange juice
2 tablespoons lemon juice
3 tablespoons honey

2 teaspoons diced chilli or
    sambal oeleck
8 preserved kumquats
3 New Zealand Kiwifruit

METHOD

Pat chicken dry and sprinkle with salt. Place portions in a baking dish just large enough to hold them in one layer. Combine the orange and lemon juice with the honey and pour over the chicken to coat well. Make sure it is well coated. Turn the chicken skin-side down. Dot the chopped chilli over the chicken. Bake uncovered at 180°C for 15 minutes. Turn the pieces over and baste well with the liquid. Bake another 15 minutes and add the kumquats, basting again. Bake a further 15-20 minutes until cooked. Add the peeled and cubed Kiwifruit, baste well and serve.

SERVES 4

MEXICAN CHICKEN WITH KIWIFRUIT AND PAWPAW SALSA

INGREDIENTS

1 large egg
3 tablespoons Mexican (chilli)
  tomato sauce
1 cup dry breadcrumbs
½ teaspoon each chilli powder,
  ground cumin, oregano
3 whole chicken breasts, skinned,
  boned and halved

25g butter
2 tablespoons oil
Salsa:
3 New Zealand Kiwifruit
½ small pawpaw (papaya)
2 tablespoons chopped coriander
  (cilantro)
2 shallots, diced

METHOD

Beat egg with Mexican tomato sauce. Combine breadcrumbs with seasonings. Dip chicken halves in egg mixture then in breadcrumbs pressing in well. Refrigerate to set coating about 30 minutes.

Melt butter and oil in a roasting pan. Add chicken, turn to coat in butter and oil. Bake at 180°C for about 25 minutes or until cooked.

Meanwhile peel and dice Kiwifruit and pawpaw. Place in a bowl with coriander and shallots. Serve with the chicken.

SERVES 8

51

STIR-FRY CHICKEN AND KIWIFRUIT

INGREDIENTS

500g boneless chicken
½ teaspoon salt
2 tablespoons cornflour
    (cornstarch)
1 teaspoon five spice powder
oil
1 clove garlic, crushed
1 red pepper (capsicum),
    thinly sliced
2 large New Zealand Kiwifruit

Sauce:
2 tablespoons Chinese vinegar
1 tablespoon light soy sauce
1 teaspoon sugar
2 teaspoons cornflour (cornstarch)
2 tablespoons cold water

METHOD

Slice chicken in thin strips. Combine salt, cornflour and five spice and toss with the chicken to coat. Place to one side.

Heat 2 tablespoons oil in a wok or frypan over high heat. Add garlic then stir-fry chicken in batches about 2-3 minutes until cooked. Drain on a paper towel. Wipe pan clean and add a tablespoon of oil and heat. Stir-fry red pepper until crisp but tender. Remove to one side. Peel and slice Kiwifruit in strips.

Pour combined sauce ingredients into the pan stirring until thickened. Add chicken and heat through. Add pepper and Kiwifruit and serve immediately.

SERVES 4-6

ASIAN KIWIFRUIT AND SPROUT SALAD

INGREDIENTS

4 New Zealand Kiwifruit
1 cup beansprouts

Satay Dressing:
1 tablespoon peanut butter
2 tablespoons oil
1 tablespoon vinegar
¼ teaspoon chilli paste (sambal oeleck)
1 teaspoon brown sugar
salt and pepper

Ginger Dressing:
½ teaspoon ginger, finely grated
1 tablespoon soy sauce
2 cloves garlic, crushed
2 tablespoons vinegar
3 tablespoons oil

METHOD

Peel and slice Kiwifruit and place on a platter with beansprouts. Chillies or diced red pepper could be used as a garnish. Serve with one of these dressings.

Satay Dressing: Combine all ingredients well and sprinkle over the salad.

Ginger Dressing: Whisk all ingredients then spoon over the salad.

SERVES 4

BLACK BEAN AND KIWIFRUIT SALAD

INGREDIENTS

2 cups cooked black beans
½ cup vinegar
½ cup sugar
¼ cup water

1 onion, diced
3 New Zealand Kiwifruit, peeled
    and diced

METHOD

Place beans in a bowl. Boil the vinegar, sugar and water until sugar is dissolved. Pour over the beans. Marinate for several hours if possible.

Meanwhile, dice onion and crisp in iced water.

Drain beans, mix with drained onion and Kiwifruit and serve.

SERVES 4-6

CHICKEN SALAD WITH NASHI AND KIWI

INGREDIENTS

125g skinless chicken breast
salt
pepper
1 teaspoon butter or margarine
1 New Zealand nashi (125g)

1 New Zealand Kiwifruit (75g)
1 tablespoon crème fraîche
    (30% fat)
lemon juice
1 handful mesclun (mixed salad)

METHOD

Season the chicken breast on both sides. Heat the butter in a coated pan. Fry the chicken breast on both sides for 3 minutes each, take it out and wrap it in aluminium foil. Meanwhile, cut the New Zealand nashi into halves, remove the core and cut the nashi into thin slices. Peel the New Zealand Kiwifruit and cut into slices. Mix the crème fraîche with some lemon juice. Season with a little salt and pepper. Take the chicken breast out of the foil and cut it into strips. Spread mesclun on a large plate. Arrange the chicken breast, the New Zealand nashi and the spring onions on it. Pour the crème fraîche dressing over it. Let it draw shortly.

SERVES 2

CHINESE CHICKEN AND KIWI SALAD

INGREDIENTS

3 New Zealand Kiwifruit
2 cups cubed cooked chicken
1 red pepper, cut into strips
1 cup thin julienne cut carrots
½ cup dry roasted, unsalted
    cashews
¼ cup thinly sliced green onions
4 cups shredded green cabbage

Honey-Soy Dressing:

⅓ cup vegetable oil
3 tablespoons light soy sauce
2 tablespoons rice wine vinegar
1 tablespoon honey
½ teaspoon ground ginger

METHOD

Peel and slice Kiwifruit into 5mm thick slices. Combine chicken, red pepper strips, carrots, cashews and green onions in medium bowl. Toss with half of Honey-Soy Dressing. To serve, divide shredded cabbage between serving plates. Drizzle evenly with remaining Honey-Soy Dressing. Spoon chicken mixture over cabbage. Garnish with Kiwifruit slices just before serving.

Honey-Soy Dressing: Combine all ingredients in small mixing bowl. Whisk until thoroughly blended. Makes ⅔ cup.

SERVES 4

CUCUMBER, KIWI AND CUMIN SALAD

INGREDIENTS

4 New Zealand Kiwifruit
2 tablespoons lemon juice
1 small onion, finely chopped
3 pickled cucumbers or gherkins,
    thinly sliced
1 stick celery, chopped
½ cup walnuts, quartered

½ teaspoon each salt, black pepper
    ground cumin
Garnish:
½ small red pepper (capsicum),
    thinly sliced
4 black olives, pitted

METHOD

Slice the peeled Kiwifruit and place in a bowl. Sprinkle with the lemon
juice. Add the onion, cucumbers, celery and walnuts. Season with salt,
pepper and cumin. Toss and chill for 30 minutes. Before serving, garnish
with strips of red pepper and the black olives.

SERVES 4

HOT NEW ZEALAND KIWIFRUIT AND BACON SALAD

INGREDIENTS

4 New Zealand Kiwifruit
8 rashers green back bacon
225g egg tagliatelle

30ml white wine vinegar
pepper

METHOD

Peel and thickly slice the Kiwifruit. Cut each slice in half. Scissor-cut the rinded bacon into 1cm (½ inch) pieces. Cook the pasta as directed on the pack. Meanwhile, dry-fry the bacon for about five minutes until crisp and golden. Add the vinegar to the pan, bring to the boil and pour over the well-drained hot pasta. Season with freshly milled pepper and fork through the Kiwifruit.

Serve accompanied by a green salad.

Note: Served straight from the pan to the plate, this dish needs little attention. Pasta should be eaten as quickly as possible after it has been cooked.

SERVES 4

KIWIFRUIT PASTA SALAD

INGREDIENTS

125g uncooked pasta
3 New Zealand Kiwifruit
½ cup black olives

Dressing:
2 tablespoons olive oil
1 tablespoon lemon juice
2 tablespoons chopped fresh basil
freshly ground black pepper

METHOD

Cook pasta in plenty of salted water until just tender. Drain.

Peel and slice Kiwifruit. Combine with pasta and black olives.

Whisk all ingredients for dressing and pour over salad.

SERVES 2-4

KIWIFRUIT SALAD IN ORANGE BLOSSOM SYRUP

INGREDIENTS

Orange Blossom Syrup:
½ cup sugar
½ cup water
rind of 1 orange, cut in
    julienne strips
2 tablespoons lemon juice

Salad:
4 New Zealand Kiwifruit
1 large banana
1 cup watermelon cubes
1 cup black grapes
1 cup strawberries

METHOD

Cook sugar, water and orange rind in a saucepan for 4 minutes, stirring. Add lemon juice and cool. Prepare fruit and place in a bowl. Pour syrup over fruit and marinate at least 1 hour. Serve with yoghurt, custard or cream.

SERVES 6

KIWIFRUIT SALAD WITH CUMIN YOGHURT

INGREDIENTS

5 New Zealand Kiwifruit, peeled
    and sliced
½ cup walnuts, optional

½ cup plain yoghurt
1 teaspoon ground cumin
dash Tabasco (hot pepper) sauce

METHOD

Place Kiwifruit in a salad bowl with walnuts if required.

Combine all other ingredients and pour over Kiwifruit before serving.

SERVES 4

KIWI GADO GADO

INGREDIENTS

2 cups sliced, blanched cabbage
   or sliced lettuce
3 potatoes, boiled, peeled and
   sliced
100g beansprouts
1 onion, sliced, optional
150g sliced carrots, blanched
4 New Zealand Kiwifruit
2 hard-boiled eggs, optional

Peanut Satay Sauce or
Kiwi Peanut Dressing:
2 New Zealand Kiwifruit
2 tablespoons each sesame oil,
   crunchy peanut butter
2 tablespoons soy sauce
1 tablespoon palm or brown sugar
1 teaspoon chopped chilli
1 tablespoon light vinegar

METHOD

Place cabbage on a large platter and top with potatoes, sprouts, onion, carrots, sliced hard-boiled eggs and Kiwifruit.

Prepare a traditional peanut Satay Sauce to serve with the salad or the Kiwi Peanut Dressing. To make, place Kiwifruit in a blender with all other ingredients and process until mixed. Serve over the salad.

SERVES 4

KIWI TABOULEH

INGREDIENTS

250g burghul or cracked wheat
3 New Zealand Kiwifruit
½ cucumber
3 tomatoes
½ onion

½ cup chopped parsley
¼ cup chopped mint
1 teaspoon salt
juice 2 lemons
2 tablespoons olive oil

METHOD

Rinse the burghul several times until the water is clean. Place in a bowl and soak in 1 cup boiling water for 1 hour. Drain.

Peel and finely dice the fruit and vegetables and combine in a bowl with herbs, salt, lemon juice and olive oil. Add to the wheat. Mix well and leave for 15 minutes. Serve on a lettuce-lined plate or in a bowl.

SERVES 6-8

NEW ZEALAND BROWN RICE SALAD

INGREDIENTS

1 cup brown rice
2 New Zealand Kiwifruit
1 New Zealand Granny Smith
   or Braeburn apple
½ cup thinly sliced celery
½ cup red pepper strips

½ cup toasted walnut pieces
¼ cup thinly sliced green onions
2 tablespoons chopped parsley
3 tablespoons sherry vinegar
2 tablespoons olive oil

METHOD

Cook rice in water according to package directions. Drain and cool. Peel Kiwifruit and cut into 5mm thick slices. Cut slices in half to form half circles. Core and dice apple into 1cm cubes. Toss rice, Kiwifruit, apple, celery, red pepper strips, walnuts, green onions and parsley. Mix together vinegar and oil; drizzle over salad. Toss to mix well. Cover and refrigerate 1-2 hours, to allow flavours to blend, before serving.

SERVES 6

SALAD OF KIWIFRUIT AND
SUN-DRIED TOMATOES

INGREDIENTS

6 New Zealand Kiwifruit
¼ cup sun-dried tomatoes,
    packed in oil

fresh basil leaves
freshly ground black pepper

METHOD

Peel and slice Kiwifruit into a salad bowl. Carefully arrange tomatoes
with the fruit. Add basil and pepper and serve.

SERVES 4

SEAFOOD COMBINATION SALAD

INGREDIENTS

500g assorted seafood, e.g. prawns,
mussels, squid (calamari)
rings, white fish

¼ cup rice or white vinegar

2 teaspoons light soy sauce

50g snow pea or beansprouts

3 spring onions, sliced

1 tablespoon finely grated ro
ginger

2 cloves garlic, crushed

2 tablespoons each sesame oi
lemon juice

3 New Zealand Kiwifruit, pe
and sliced

METHOD

Prepare the seafood, shell the prawns, cut fish in cubes, trim musse
combine with squid rings. Mix the vinegar and soy sauce and pou
the fish. Mix gently so liquid is well dispersed. Refrigerate for at
hour. Steam seafood until just cooked.

Combine with all remaining ingredients except Kiwifruit. Allow fla
to mellow for an hour then add the Kiwifruit and serve.

SERVES 4

SESAME SPROUT KIWI SALAD

INGREDIENTS

2 cups fresh beansprouts
4 New Zealand Kiwifruit
1 tablespoon each sesame seed
oil, salad oil, toasted
crushed sesame seeds
3 tablespoons light soy sauce

1 clove garlic, crushed
2 spring onions (scallions), finely
chopped
1 teaspoon honey
dash chilli powder or cayenne

METHOD

Bring a large saucepan of water to the boil and blanch beansprouts briefly.
Do not overcook. Remove and refresh in cold water. Drain well.

Peel and slice Kiwifruit in matchstick strips. Combine with beansprouts.
Mix all other ingredients for dressing and toss with sprouts and Kiwifruit.
Chill.

SERVES 6

SUB-TROPICAL CHICKEN SALAD

INGREDIENTS

Dressing:

6 tablespoons olive oil
3 tablespoons cider vinegar
1 teaspoon French mustard
salt and pepper
1 tablespoon brown sugar

Salad:

600g cooked, boned, chicken
½ pawpaw (papaya), sliced
3 New Zealand Kiwifruit, peeled
   and sliced
2 spring onions (scallions), sliced
   diagonally

METHOD

Whisk all ingredients for dressing.

Break up chicken and slice if required. Place on a serving plate with fruits
and onion. Drizzle with dressing before serving.

SERVES 6

TRI-COLOUR NEW ZEALAND SALAD

INGREDIENTS

4 New Zealand Kiwifruit
1 large tomato
1 cucumber
2 avocados

fresh basil sprigs
juice of 1 orange (½ cup)
1 teaspoon balsamic vinegar
½ teaspoon Dijon-style mustard

METHOD

Wash and trim ends from Kiwifruit. Cut into 5mm thick slices. Cut tomato into wedges. Slice cucumber. Peel and slice avocados. Arrange ingredients equally on four salad plates. Garnish with basil sprigs. Whisk together orange juice, vinegar and mustard until thoroughly combined. Drizzle over salad to serve.

SERVES 4

ALMOND MOUSSE WITH KIWIFRUIT

INGREDIENTS

50g ground toasted almonds
½ teaspoon each vanilla,
    almond essence
1½ cups medium custard
3 teaspoons powdered gelatine
3 egg whites

2 tablespoons sugar
¾ cup cream
Sauce:
4-5 New Zealand Kiwifruit
2 tablespoons lemon juice
3 tablespoons sugar

METHOD

Mix the almonds, vanilla and almond essences in a bowl and combine with the custard.

Combine the gelatine with 3 tablespoons water. Stand for 5 minutes then dissolve over hot water. Stir into the almond mixture. Whisk the egg whites and fold in the sugar. Beat the cream until thick. Fold the egg whites and cream into the almond mixture and stir carefully until well blended. Spoon into a decorative dish or serve in individual dessert dishes. Refrigerate to set. Peel and chop the Kiwifruit. Place in a food processor with lemon juice and sugar. Process until just smooth. Pass through a conical sieve to remove seeds. When the mousse has set, pour the sauce over the top. Decorate with strawberries and serve chilled.

SERVES 6-8

BAKED APPLE WITH NEW ZEALAND KIWIFRUIT SAUCE

INGREDIENTS

250ml orange juice
40g sugar
¼ vanilla pod
4 baking apples
30g butter

3 New Zealand Kiwifruit (each
    approx. 100g)
3 tablespoons white wine
pinch of cinnamon
25g slivered almonds

METHOD

Combine the orange juice, sugar and scraped out vanilla pod in a heavy saucepan and boil until syrupy. Peel and core the apples. Brush a small, oven-proof dish with butter, add the apples and pour the orange syrup over them. Then add the remaining butter. Bake the apples at 200°C in a preheated oven for approximately 15 minutes or until tender. Meanwhile, peel the Kiwifruit and cut into pieces. Add the wine and cinnamon and put into a blender. Roast the slivered almonds in a heavy bottomed pan, without adding fat. Remove the apples from the dish and place on warmed plates. Pour some Kiwifruit purée over each apple and garnish with almonds.

Serve with whipped cream for a dessert or with Kiwifruit purée only to accompany all game dishes.

SERVES 4

BANANA KIWIFRUIT ROYALE

INGREDIENTS

3 New Zealand Kiwifruit
1-2 tablespoons sugar
25g butter
4 small bananas

½ cup pecans or walnuts
juice of 1 small orange
2-3 tablespoons brandy, optional
¾ cup cream

METHOD

Peel and slice the Kiwifruit. Sprinkle with sugar.

Melt the butter in a frying pan and add the peeled and sliced bananas. Stir-fry gently for 1 minute then add the nuts. Stir well. Pour in the orange juice and sizzle for a minute. Add the brandy and when warmed, carefully ignite.

When the flames die, pour in the cream and simmer 1 minute. Add the Kiwifruit and serve. Good with chocolate or vanilla ice cream.

SERVES 4

BLACK FOREST KIWI CAKE

INGREDIENTS

1 x 18cm (7") light but rich
    chocolate cake

Syrup:
½ cup sugar
¾ cup water
4 tablespoons Kirsch
2 New Zealand Kiwifruit, peeled
    and sliced

Filling and Topping:
1½ cups chilled cream for
    whipping
½ cup icing (confectioners') sugar
2 tablespoons Kirsch
2-3 New Zealand Kiwifruit

Garnish:
glacé cherries
chocolate curls

METHOD

Slice cake to make 3-4 rounds.

Prepare syrup by dissolving sugar in water and boiling for 5 minutes. Add
the Kiwifruit and simmer 2 minutes. Cool and add the Kirsch.

Skewer the cakes in several places and sprinkle evenly with the syrup.

Place one round of cake on plate and cover with poached Kiwifruit slices.

Whip the cream with icing sugar and add some more Kirsch. Spread some
cream over the cake. Top with another layer, adding Kiwifruit and more
cream. Repeat if there is another layer of cake. Spread top and sides with
whipped cream.

Garnish the top with Kiwifruit and glacé cherries. Press chocolate curls
onto the sides of the cake.

SERVES 6-8

CHOCOHOLIC MOUSSE AND FRUIT SALAD COULIS

INGREDIENTS

Chocoholic Mousse:
1 tablespoon orange liqueur
3 eggs, separated
200g dark chocolate, chopped
¾ cup cream, whipped

Fruit Salad Coulis:
4 New Zealand Kiwifruit
½ cup pineapple juice or
    passionfruit pulp
½ cup each melon balls,
    berries or grapes

METHOD

Beat liqueur into egg yolks until well mixed. Melt chopped chocolate in microwave on high (100%) power, about 2 minutes, or over hot water. Cool completely stirring until shiny. Whisk in egg mixture. Slowly fold in whipped cream.

Beat egg whites until stiff, lightly fold into mousse until no streaks remain. Spoon into 6-8 round moulds. Chill until firm then freeze until required.

To unmould, dip into warm water and invert onto serving plates.

To prepare coulis, purée three Kiwifruit, sieve and add juice or passionfruit pulp. Prepare small melon balls from remaining Kiwifruit. Spoon coulis around the mousse and top with kiwi and melon balls and berries. Papaya (pawpaw) could also be used.

SERVES 6-8

74

EXOTIC FRUIT SALAD

INGREDIENTS

1 New Zealand Kiwifruit (75g)
125g dark seedless grapes
1 New Zealand nashi (150g)

2 teaspoons honey
lemon juice
mint

METHOD

Peel the New Zealand Kiwifruit, cut it into slices and halves. Wash the grapes and cut them into halves. Divide the New Zealand nashi into eight parts, remove the kernels and cut into thin slices. Mix the fruit. Mix the honey with the lemon juice and pour it over the fruit. Finally, spread some mint leaves over it.

SERVES 2

FRUIT PLATTER

INGREDIENTS

250g watermelon
2 oranges
1 small bunch grapes

4 New Zealand Kiwifruit
1 apple
1 pear

METHOD

Cut watermelon in wedges. Peel and segment the oranges. Wash grapes, peel and slice Kiwifruit. Peel apple and pear and cut in attractive shapes. Arrange attractively on a platter. Serve as a sweet ending to dinner.

SERVES 6

FRUIT SALAD SKEWERS WITH LEMON SUGAR

INGREDIENTS

4 New Zealand Kiwifruit
450g prepared fruits e.g. pawpaw
   (papaya), melon, pineapple,
   grapes, strawberries

Lemon Sugar:
½ cup sugar
grated rind of 1 lemon
1-2 teaspoons lemon juice

METHOD

Peel Kiwifruit and cut in quarters. Thread on skewers alternately with cubed pawpaw and melon.

To prepare sugar, stir rind into sugar adding enough to give a strong flavour. Stir in a little lemon juice, enough that the granules can still be sprinkled.

SERVES 4

KIWI AND TOASTED ALMOND GELATO

INGREDIENTS

3-4 New Zealand Kiwifruit
70g slivered almonds
½ cup sugar

1 teaspoon vanilla essence
¾ cup milk

METHOD

Peel and slice Kiwifruit. Mash and sieve or process in a food processor until well mashed. Sieve if desired. Lightly toast the almonds then grind the nuts finely.

Add sugar to the Kiwifruit with vanilla, milk and nuts. Freeze in an ice cream maker preferably, or in a deep freeze until almost solid. Beat well then return to freezer until solid. Thaw in refrigerator 10 minutes before serving.

SERVES 4-5

KIWI BIRTHDAY CAKE

INGREDIENTS

1 prepared 20cm sponge or
Sponge Cake:
4 eggs
¾ cup caster (superfine) sugar
1¼ cups self-raising flour
1 teaspoon butter
3 tablespoons hot water

Topping:
¼ cup sugar
¼ cup orange juice
1 cup cream, whipped
3 New Zealand Kiwifruit
julienne lemon rind

METHOD

To prepare cake, beat eggs until light and thick. Gradually beat in the sugar until thick and sugar is completely dissolved. Sift flour several times; melt butter in hot water.

Sift dry ingredients over egg mixture, fold in, then working quickly, fold in the butter mixture.

Pour into a greased and floured deep 20cm (8") cake pan. Bake at 180°C for about 25 minutes until cake shrinks slightly from sides of pan. Turn onto a cake cooler. Leave until cold.

To prepare topping, boil sugar and orange juice until sugar is dissolved. Cut cake in three equal rounds. Place base on a serving plate and sprinkle with half the orange mixture. Spread with whipped cream. Top with middle layer of cake and 2 thickly sliced Kiwifruit. Top with final layer of cake, sprinkle with juice then spread with more cream. Place rounds of Kiwifruit on top and around the sides of the cake. Place candles in centres of Kiwifruit to make the birthday cake. Sprinkle centre of cake with julienne lemon.

SERVES 6-8

KIWI CARAMEL

INGREDIENTS

1 cup hot water

1 cup sugar

3 eggs

1 egg yolk

¼ cup caster (superfine) sugar

2 cups milk

1 teaspoon vanilla essence

4 New Zealand Kiwifruit, peeled

METHOD

Combine water and sugar in the saucepan and stir until dissolved over low heat. Bring to boil and boil rapidly until golden. Pour into 6 individual ramekins. Allow to cool and harden.

Meanwhile beat the eggs, egg yolk and sugar. Heat the milk and whisk into egg mixture with vanilla. Strain into a jug and divide equally between the dishes.

Place ramekins in a baking dish with enough water to come half-way up the side of the pan. Bake at 150°C for about 30 minutes until custard is set. Cool and chill.

Meanwhile chop and purée the Kiwifruit. Sieve to remove seeds. To serve, invert each caramel and lift onto a serving plate and spoon the coulis of Kiwifruit around the edge. Use extra Kiwifruit to make small balls if desired.

SERVES 6

KIWI BROWNIE SUNDAE

INGREDIENTS

6 New Zealand Kiwifruit
½ cup orange marmalade

6 brownies
6 scoops vanilla ice cream

METHOD

Peel and quarter 3 Kiwifruit. Place in food processor with metal blade in place; pulse on and off until fruit is puréed but seeds are not crushed. Melt marmalade in small saucepan over low heat. Stir into Kiwifruit purée. Chill sauce until thick. To assemble sundaes, peel and slice remaining Kiwifruit into 5mm thick slices. Cut slices in half to form half rounds. Place 1 brownie on each serving plate. Top each with 1 scoop ice cream. Garnish with Kiwifruit slices and drizzle with Kiwifruit sauce.

SERVES 6

KIWIFRUIT AND BLUEBERRY PIZZA

INGREDIENTS

4 small pita rounds (popettes)
250g light cream cheese
2 teaspoons Drambuie or other
    liqueur
1 tablespoon caster (superfine)
    sugar

3 New Zealand Kiwifruit, peeled
    and diced
150g fresh or frozen blueberries

METHOD

Divide pita bread in half to make eight rounds. Lightly toast under a grill.

Combine cream cheese with liqueur and caster sugar. Spread on cooled pita rounds. Top with Kiwifruit and blueberries.

SERVES 8

KIWIFRUIT KATAIFI

INGREDIENTS

375g kataifi pastry
150g butter, melted
6 New Zealand Kiwifruit
1 cup walnuts, chopped
¼ cup honey
¼ cup sugar

Syrup:
½ cup water
½ cup sugar
1 tablespoon lemon juice

METHOD

Remove pastry from packet and shake loose. Cut pastry in 6 x 12 cm (2½" x 5") lengths. Brush with melted butter. Peel and dice the Kiwifruit and combine with walnuts, honey and sugar. Place a teaspoon of the fruit filling at one end of each pastry strip and roll up firmly.

Place in a greased oven dish in a single layer. Brush with melted butter. Bake at 160°C for one hour until golden.

Make the syrup by heating water and dissolving the sugar. Add the juice and simmer for 5 minutes. Pour over the rolls. Cover until cool. Serve at room temperature.

SERVES 8-10

KIWIFRUIT MUFFINS

INGREDIENTS

1 cup bran flakes
½ cup brown sugar, loosely
    packed
1 cup plain flour
1 teaspoon baking powder
½ teaspoon each, salt, ground
    cinnamon

1 egg, lightly beaten
1 tablespoon oil
1 teaspoon baking soda
½ cup milk
2 New Zealand Kiwifruit, peeled
    and chopped

METHOD

Place flakes and sugar in a bowl and stir well. Sift in flour, baking powder and cinnamon. Combine egg, oil and the baking soda dissolved in milk. Pour into dry ingredients with Kiwifruit and stir until just combined.

Spoon into lightly greased muffin pans until three-quarters full.

Bake at 200°C for 15 minutes until golden and cooked.

SERVES 6-8

KIWIFRUIT SUNDAE

INGREDIENTS

1 litre vanilla ice cream
5 New Zealand Kiwifruit
1 tablespoon sugar

1 tablespoon concentrated orange
  juice
garnish: strawberries or grapes

METHOD

Prepare small scoops of ice cream and return to freezer to set.

Peel, purée and sieve 3 Kiwifruit adding sugar and juice to taste. Peel and slice remaining fruit.

Pile ice cream in four sundae dishes and add sliced fruit and berries to garnish. Serve with the purée poured over the top.

SERVES 4

KIWIFRUIT WAFFLES

INGREDIENTS

2 cups plain flour
½ teaspoon salt
1 teaspoon baking powder
2 eggs
1½ cups milk

2 tablespoons water
2 tablespoons oil
1 tablespoon sugar
4 New Zealand Kiwifruit

METHOD

Sift dry ingredients. Beat eggs lightly. Add milk, water, oil and sugar.
Gradually stir into the flour until smooth.

Peel and dice 2 Kiwifruit and add to the mixture. Pour 3-4 tablespoons
batter on to preheated waffle plates. Cook until golden.

Serve with remaining Kiwifruit, peeled and sliced. Fried bacon and syrup
(maple or corn) could also be served with the waffles.

MAKES ABOUT 12 WAFFLES

KIWIFRUIT WITH POACHED SWEET POTATO

INGREDIENTS

¼ cup sugar
⅓ cup water
2cm knob root ginger

325g kumara (sweet potato)
3 New Zealand Kiwifruit
1 orange, segmented

METHOD

Dissolve sugar in water. Peel and thinly slice the ginger. Add to syrup.

Peel and slice kumara and steam or boil until tender. Add to the syrup and boil 2 minutes. Cool.

Peel and slice Kiwifruit. Place in 4 serving bowls with orange segments and kumara. Pour a little syrup over the fruits.

SERVES 4

KIWI MELBA

INGREDIENTS

6-8 New Zealand Kiwifruit
1 cup sugar
½ cup water
1 vanilla pod

4 scoops vanilla ice cream
1 cup raspberry purée
3 tablespoons red currant jelly,
    melted

METHOD

Peel the Kiwifruit and halve. Make a syrup by boiling sugar and water
with vanilla pod. Cool slightly and pour over Kiwifruit. Chill.

Place scoops of ice cream in a serving plate and top with Kiwifruit. Coat
with raspberry purée combined with red currant jelly.

SERVES 4

KIWI PANCAKES

INGREDIENTS

2 cups buttermilk baking mix
1 cup milk
2 eggs
¼ teaspoon ground nutmeg

4 New Zealand Kiwifruit
powdered sugar, for dusting
strawberry jam

METHOD

Beat together baking mix, milk, eggs and nutmeg until smooth. Wash and trim ends from Kiwifruit. Dice fruit and stir into pancake batter. Spoon approximately ½ cup batter onto lightly greased, heated griddle. Cook until edges are dry and bubbles appear. Flip pancakes and cook until golden brown. Arrange pancakes on serving plates. Sprinkle with powdered sugar and drizzle with strawberry jam. Makes 8 x 12cm (5 inch) pancakes.

SERVES 4

KIWI TIRAMISU

INGREDIENTS

3 New Zealand Kiwifruit
3 egg yolks
½ cup icing sugar
    (confectioners'/powdered)
¼ cup Tia Maria
250g light cream cheese

1½ cups cream (whipping)
¼ teaspoon vanilla essence
200g sponge cake
1¼ cups strong coffee
1 tablespoon cocoa

METHOD

Line a 20cm (8") glass bowl with peeled and sliced Kiwifruit. Beat egg yolks with icing sugar and Tia Maria over warm water until light. Cool.

Slowly beat the cream cheese. Beat into the egg yolk mixture. Whip the cream, gradually adding vanilla. Fold into egg yolk mixture. Cut sponge into fingers (or use lady fingers). Dip the fingers into the coffee to just moisten. Place a layer of fingers in the base of a large bowl. Spoon the cheese mixture over. Cover with more fingers. Repeat the layers. Sprinkle the surface with cocoa.

SERVES 4

LIGHT KIWI CHEESECAKE

INGREDIENTS

1 x 20cm biscuit crumb crust
3 New Zealand Kiwifruit, diced
¼ cup sugar
2 tablespoons lemon juice
4 teaspoons powdered gelatine
2 tablespoons cold water
2 eggs

½ cup sugar
500g cottage cheese
1 cup yoghurt
½ teaspoon vanilla essence
2 New Zealand Kiwifruit, extra
    diced

METHOD

Place diced Kiwifruit, sugar and lemon juice in small saucepan. Simmer gently until thick. Cool.

Soften gelatine in cold water.

Separate eggs, place egg yolks and ¼ cup sugar in a double boiler. Whisk gently over boiling water until thick and creamy. Add softened gelatine. Whisk to melt. Cool.

Place cottage cheese and yoghurt in a food processor and process until smooth.

Add cooled egg and gelatine mixture, essence and mix well. Stir in Kiwifruit mixture.

Beat egg whites until stiff, gradually add remaining ¼ cup sugar and beat until shiny. Fold into cottage cheese and yoghurt mixture. Pour carefully into prepared crumb crust. Refrigerate until set. Place diced Kiwifruit on top before serving.

SERVES ABOUT 10

MELON FRUIT BASKET

INGREDIENTS

1 small honeydew melon
425g can lychees
½ cup cubed rock melon
   (cantaloupe) or pawpaw
   (papaya)

1 cup watermelon balls
2-3 New Zealand Kiwifruit, peeled
   and sliced
2-3 tablespoons orange juice

METHOD

Remove top from honeydew melon and hollow out the flesh leaving the thick shell. Remove seeds and dice flesh to use in melon basket.

Prepare all other fruit. Arrange attractively in the melon. Sprinkle with a little orange juice.

SERVES 3

MELON, KIWI AND ROSEWATER

INGREDIENTS

1 large cantaloupe (rock melon)
   or Persian melon
4 New Zealand Kiwifruit
½ teaspoon salt

½ cup sugar
2 tablespoons lemon juice
3 teaspoons rosewater
crushed or shaved ice, optional

METHOD

Prepare melon balls from the seeded melon. Place in a deep bowl with any juice from the melon. Peel Kiwifruit and make into balls. Add to the melon. Toss with salt.

Combine the sugar and lemon juice and heat to dissolve the sugar. Add the rosewater. Cool and sprinkle over the melon mixture. Cover and chill in the refrigerator.

To serve, spoon into individual dishes. Top each portion with ice if desired.

SERVES 4

NEW ZEALAND KIWIFRUIT AND LEMON SYLLABUB

INGREDIENTS

4 New Zealand Kiwifruit
12 tiny ratafia biscuits
150ml carton double cream, chilled

75ml sweet white wine
45ml lemon curd
4 small strawberries, mint sprigs, optional

METHOD

Peel the Kiwifruit. Cut in thin slices and use as many as required to line four stemmed glasses or a large bowl. Chop the remainder, combine with crushed ratafias and spoon into the base. Whisk together the chilled cream, wine and lemon curd until thick and floppy. Spoon into glasses. Chill for about 2 hours.

Note: Quick and easy to make, this kind of syllabub never fails to delight the palate. The bouquet – achieved with a slice of New Zealand Kiwifruit, strawberry rose and mint sprig – makes a memorable dessert. At best served lightly chilled.

SERVES 4

NEW ZEALAND KIWIFRUIT EN CROUTE

INGREDIENTS

175g plain flour
75g butter
25g caster (superfine) sugar
1 orange

4 New Zealand Kiwifruit
1 egg, beaten
150ml carton double cream
15ml Grand Marnier

METHOD

Rub together the flour and butter until the mixture resembles fine breadcrumbs. Add the sugar and half the grated rind of the orange. Bind mixture together into a firm dough with 30ml (2 tablespoons) orange juice. Chill. Peel Kiwifruit carefully. Roll pastry out into 4 rectangles approx. 23 x 12.5cm (9" x 5"). Wrap the Kiwifruit in pastry, sealing the ends with water. Decorate with pastry leaves made from the trimmings. Make a hole in the centre of each parcel. Brush with beaten egg. Bake at 200°C (400°F) for about 15 minutes until golden brown. Serve warm accompanied by orange cream – whip the cream until the floppy stage, fold in remaining orange rind, 15ml (1 tablespoon) orange juice and Grand Marnier. Whip again lightly.

SERVES 4

NEW ZEALAND KIWIFRUIT SUPER-CUP

INGREDIENTS

6 New Zealand Kiwifruit (each of 100g)
1 tablespoon orange marmalade
1 tablespoon orange liqueur
½ teaspoon vanilla sugar
6 large vanilla ice cream balls
6 large balls of pistachio/strawberry ice cream

METHOD

Peel the Kiwifruit, cut two of them lengthwise into halves and horizontally into slices. Cut the remaining four Kiwifruit into pieces and mash them with a fork (do not purée them), and mix with the orange marmalade, the orange liqueur and the vanilla sugar. Fill the differently coloured ice cream balls into well chilled glasses. Decorate the spaces in between the ice cream balls with the halved Kiwifruit slices so that the lighter central parts show. Pour the prepared Kiwifruit sauce with a tablespoon over the ice cream and serve immediately.

SERVES 4

SUMMER AMBROSIA WITH RASPBERRY SAUCE

INGREDIENTS

2 oranges
1 cup strawberries
4 New Zealand Kiwifruit
raspberry sauce
¼ cup toasted, shredded coconut

Raspberry Sauce:
175g frozen, slightly sweetened
    raspberries, thawed
1 tablespoon raspberry or other
    fruit liqueur, optional

METHOD

Peel and slice oranges. Rinse and slice strawberries. Wash and trim ends
from Kiwifruit; cut into 5mm slices. Spoon Raspberry Sauce evenly onto
serving plates. Divide and arrange fruit on plates. Sprinkle with toasted
coconut to serve.

Raspberry Sauce: Whirl raspberries and liqueur in blender until smooth.
Strain, if desired, to remove seeds. Makes ½ cup. May be made one day
ahead and kept covered, in refrigerator.

SERVES 4

TROPICAL KIWI ICE

INGREDIENTS

4 New Zealand Kiwifruit   ½ cup sugar
1 cup cubed melon (honeydew or   1 teaspoon grated lemon rind
   cantaloupe)

METHOD

Wash and trim ends from Kiwifruit. Cut into cubes and put into food processor with metal blade in place. Add remaining ingredients. Process just until smooth, being careful not to crush seeds. Pour mixture into a 20cm (8 inch) metal pan. Cover with foil; freeze until firm. Remove from freezer; let stand 10 minutes. Break into small pieces and put into food processor with metal blade in place. Process until smooth. Pack into plastic or cardboard container and cover. Return to freezer. Alternatively, freeze in ice cream freezer, following manufacturer's instructions. Serve by scooping.

SERVES 4

TROPICAL WAFFLES

INGREDIENTS

4 New Zealand Kiwifruit
¼ cup butter
1 cup maple syrup

¼ cup pineapple juice concentrate
4 waffles

METHOD

Peel and slice Kiwifruit into 5mm thick slices. Melt butter in medium saucepan. Whisk in maple syrup; bring mixture to a boil. Remove from heat; whisk in pineapple juice concentrate. Keep syrup warm. Prepare waffles. To serve, divide waffles between serving plates. Top with Kiwifruit slices. Drizzle with warm syrup just before serving.

SERVES 4

FROZEN FRUIT KEBABS

INGREDIENTS

2 New Zealand Kiwifruit
4 whole strawberries
8 melon balls (cantaloupe,
    watermelon or honeydew)

4 x 20cm bamboo skewers
mint sprigs, optional

METHOD

Wash and trim ends from Kiwifruit. Cut each into four wedges. Arrange Kiwifruit, strawberries, and melon balls on skewers. Freeze until firm. To serve, place one skewer of fruit in each glass. Pour over your favourite fruit drink and garnish with mint sprigs, if desired, or try one of the following combinations:

- Cranberry juice and sparkling water
- Orange juice and lemon-lime soda
- Chilled fruit tea and lemonade

SERVES 4

HOT NEW ZEALAND KIWIFRUIT PUNCH

INGREDIENTS

3 peeled New Zealand Kiwifruit,
   sliced
1 heaped teaspoon sugar-candy
100ml boiling water

1 lime peel spiral
40ml white rum
20ml lime juice

METHOD

Moisten the rim of a tall glass and dip it into the sugar. Add the sugar-candy. Put the Kiwifruit slices and the lime peel spiral as decoration in the glass. Pour in the hot water over a silver spoon and add the white rum (heated in a scoop over a flame) and the lime juice. Serve immediately.

SERVES 1

KIWIANA SMOOTHIE

INGREDIENTS

2 New Zealand Kiwifruit
1 banana
½ cup sweetened yoghurt

½ cup orange juice
sugar to taste

METHOD

Peel and chop Kiwifruit. Place in a blender or food processor with the peeled banana and add the yoghurt, juice and sugar to taste. Blend until smooth. Pour into two glasses to serve. Serve over ice if desired.

SERVES 2

KIWI CAFE

INGREDIENTS

1 New Zealand Kiwifruit   ¾ cup strong coffee, chilled
1 tablespoon brown sugar   ¼ cup milk, chilled

METHOD

Peel, chop and purée the Kiwifruit. Sieve to remove seeds.

Place in the base of a long glass and add sugar. Carefully pour coffee onto the Kiwifruit to give two layers. Add the milk.

SERVES 1

KIWI FROSTY

INGREDIENTS

225g light cream cheese
2 tablespoons Kiwifruit topping
3 New Zealand Kiwifruit, peeled
 and sliced

1 cup apricot yoghurt
1 cup limeade or lemonade (7 Up)

METHOD

Place cream cheese, Kiwifruit topping, Kiwifruit and yoghurt in a food
processor or blender and process until smooth. Add limeade and continue
processing until smooth. Pour over ice to serve.

SERVES 4-6

KIWIFRUIT SPRITZER

INGREDIENTS

3 New Zealand Kiwifruit
2 tablespoons sugar

1 cup cubed watermelon
¾ cup Club soda, chilled

METHOD

Cut 3 rounds of Kiwifruit to use as garnishes for the sides of the glasses. Combine remaining Kiwifruit and sugar in a food processor briefly. Pour in a container and chill. Purée the watermelon until smooth and chill separately.

Just before serving combine watermelon with the soda – add soda slowly to watermelon as it will froth up. Drinks can be served with fruit purées mixed together or poured separately into glasses, Kiwifruit on the bottom and watermelon on top.

SERVES 3

KIWI WHIP

INGREDIENTS

2 large New Zealand Kiwifruit   crushed ice
1-2 tablespoons sugar or honey   1-2 tablespoons egg white,
  optional

METHOD

Peel and chop Kiwifruit. Place in a blender or food processor with the sugar and process until smooth. Do not crush the seeds. Sieve.

Return to the blender. Blend on a high speed with ¼ cup ice and the egg white. Pour over ice to serve.

SERVES 2

LONG TALL KIWI

INGREDIENTS

2 large New Zealand Kiwifruit   1 cup milk
2 tablespoons sugar   ice blocks

METHOD

Peel and chop Kiwifruit. Place in a blender or food processor with sugar. Blend until smooth but do not crush the seeds. Add the milk and blend until well combined. Pour into long Pilsener glasses and add 2-3 ice blocks to each glass. Serve and drink immediately with a straw.

SERVES 2

MADE IN THE SHADE

INGREDIENTS

3 New Zealand Kiwifruit   1½ cups cubed watermelon
2 tablespoons sugar, optional

METHOD

Cut 2 rounds of Kiwifruit to use as a garnish. Combine remaining Kiwifruit and sugar in a food processor or blender briefly. Chill. Purée the watermelon and chill separately.

Pour Kiwifruit into two glasses and top up with watermelon. Garnish each with a round of Kiwifruit and a paper umbrella.

SERVES 2

NEW ZEALAND KIWIFRUIT RUM

INGREDIENTS

350g sugar
1 vanilla pod
125ml water
2 tablespoons lemon juice

700ml bottle white rum (38%)
1kg red grapes
10 New Zealand Kiwifruit
  (each 100g)

METHOD

Put the sugar into a pan. Cut the vanilla pod, scrape out the inside and put it together with the scrapings with the sugar. Add the water and bring it to the boil, stirring continuously for 10 minutes. Take the pan off the heat, add the lemon juice to the sugar syrup quickly, so that it does not become firm. Let it cool, set in another pan of water and stir now and again. When it has cooled slightly, add the rum bit by bit. Wash the grapes, let them drain. Peel the Kiwifruit and cut them into approx. 3mm thick slices. Make layers of the fruit in a 3 litre glass rum pot, starting with the Kiwifruit slices. Pour the rum-sugar mixture over it through a sieve. Put a small plate on the fruit so that they do not reach the surface and change colour. The Kiwifruit rum pot tastes good with ice cream and all cream dishes. The drained fruit can be used as a decoration for cakes, the juice can be served with sparkling wine as a long drink.

STRAWBERRY AND
KIWIFRUIT COOLER

INGREDIENTS

1 cup strawberries, hulled
2 New Zealand Kiwifruit, peeled
   and chopped

½-¾ cup orange juice
ice cubes

METHOD

Place strawberries and Kiwifruit into a blender with ½ cup orange juice.
Blend until quite smooth. May be strained if desired. Add extra juice if
too thick. Pour over ice to serve.

SERVES 3

INDEX

INDEX (cont.)